The DEVIL WALKS

Anne Fine

OXFORD
UNIVERSITY PRESS

OXFORD
UNIVERSITY PRESS

Great Clarendon Street, Oxford OX2 6DP

Oxford University Press is a department of the University of Oxford.
It furthers the University's objective of excellence in research,
scholarship, and education by publishing worldwide in

Oxford   New York

Auckland   Cape Town   Dar es Salaam   Hong Kong   Karachi
Kuala Lumpur   Madrid   Melbourne   Mexico City   Nairobi
New Delhi   Shanghai   Taipei   Toronto

With offices in

Argentina   Austria   Brazil   Chile   Czech Republic   France   Greece
Guatemala   Hungary   Italy   Japan   Poland   Portugal   Singapore
South Korea   Switzerland   Thailand   Turkey   Ukraine   Vietnam

Oxford is a registered trade mark of Oxford University Press
in the UK and in certain other countries

British Library Cataloguing in Publication Data

Data available

ISBN 978 019 913801 2

10 9 8 7 6

Typeset in India by TNQ Books and Journals Pvt. Ltd.
Printed by CPI Group (UK) Ltd, Croydon CR0 4YY

Acknowledgements

Extract from a review by Mal Peet of *The Devil Walks* by Anne Fine, *The Guardian*,
8.7.2011, copyright © Guardian News & Media 2011, reprinted by permission of
GNM Ltd.

The Publisher would like to thank Jenny Roberts for writing the Activity section.

Cover image © The Marsden Archive / Alamy

Artwork by Robin Lawrie

CONTENTS

What the Author Says

I love adapting my own novels into plays. I'd hate to be responsible for anyone else's work. I'd imagine them hovering constantly over my shoulder, begging me, 'Oh, please don't take out that! No, don't change that!'

But what works in a novel so often doesn't work in a dramatic reading, or on a stage. If it's my own work, then I know I can be ruthless. I feel quite free to slash out whole chunks, and twist scenes round so everything works better. Sometimes I'll give a speech to someone different. I'll do away with complicated subplots, and tinker with the timing of the story.

I'll do whatever works.

Only two things must stay the same. One is the mood of the work. The other is the characterization. *The Devil Walks* is a gothic tale, set long ago. Mostly I write realistic novels, set in the present day. But suddenly I felt an urge to write a brooding and malevolent chiller thriller, with a real villain, and this was it. I hope the tone of the work remains the same in this, the play version.

And certainly there are no changes in the characters. Daniel is still the boy he is in the book – well meaning and determined, if horribly confused by all the mysteries surrounding him. His mother, stiff, tragic and mysterious, remains the same. And so does Captain Severn, a man so mercurial that Daniel cannot fathom his true nature.

I've tried to offer ways to tame some of the action to suit the average stage. I reckon you'd have to be the director of the National Theatre to want to show a young boy climbing down a sixty feet high coil of ivy or a furiously dancing devil doll bursting from a kitchen range to burn to ashes on a flagstone floor. A great house levelled to the ground by fire can be a little tricky! I know how clever stage effects can be. But still I've tried to make it just a little easier. (Feel free to be inventive.)

What also pleases me is knowing that, because of this playscript, the original book will reach more readers. For anyone keen on drama, here's something fresh. But so many people who aren't drawn to novels happily tackle scenes – even the whole story – from play versions in Drama or English classes. And often after that they spot the full book on a library shelf, and think, 'I know that. We did that in school.' They have a go, and find that getting through it is easier than they thought because they know the story.

And then I have another reader. Excellent!

Anne Fine

About the Author

Anne Fine claims that she cannot remember any time when she could not read. Anne started at infants' school aged three, and learned to read along with all the others in the class, who were two years older. At seven, the primary school thought her too young to attend, so she had what she has called 'a blissful reading year', let off most lessons and allowed to creep into the head teacher's study and borrow whatever books she chose. Since then, she has never stopped reading. Anne claims she still spends at least as much time reading as writing. 'Show me the writer who's stopped bothering to read,' she says, 'and I'll show you the writer I won't be bothering to read much longer.'

Anne attended Northampton High School for Girls, and went on to study History and Politics at Warwick University. She says she was always perfectly content as a reader, and only began to write because one day it was impossible to reach the library due to a blizzard. With nothing fresh in the house to read, Anne sat down at the kitchen table to write a book of her own, and never stopped. She has now published over 60 novels, including eight for adults, and compiled three classic anthologies of poetry. Her work has been translated into over 40 languages.

Anne is considered one of Britain's most distinguished writers for young people, having twice won the coveted Carnegie Medal, alongside two Whitbread/Costa Awards, the Guardian, Smarties and Nestlé Awards, and many other prizes. She was twice voted Children's Author of the Year. Adaptations of her books *Bill's New Frock* and *Goggle-Eyes* have been screened by the BBC, and her novel *Madame Doubtfire* was adapted for film under the title *Mrs Doubtfire*.

Anne became Children's Laureate in 2001 and set up a website of freely downloadable modern bookplates (www. myhomelibrary.org). In 2003 she became a Fellow of the Royal Society of Literature and was awarded an OBE. Anne has two grown up daughters, and lives in County Durham with her partner Richard and an enormous hairy dog called Lulu. Her website is www.annefine.co.uk.

A Note on Staging

The Devil Walks takes place a hundred years or so ago in two main settings. The first is the tiny town where Dr Marlow lives with his family. The second is the strange and isolated old house, High Gates, where Daniel is sent to stay. Clearly, the costumes should be vaguely within the period. Daniel will probably wear a jacket and knickerbockers. The ladies will wear long skirts.

The play will take some quite inventive staging, not least because, through necessity, we have a range of indoor and outdoor scenes. At no point is the doll's house shown as being physically moved, so the first act sets could be designed with it in the same position in both. Lighting, backdrops, impressions of hedges, etc. are obvious solutions for the outdoor scenes. Some props (i.e. the stone eagles on the gates, and even the front of the house in Act 2, Scene 2) are optional, since Daniel could simply point at them as though just offstage. The double-ended doll, on its appearance in the third act, will be attached to transparent threads (like plastic fishing wire), in order for it to seem to be moving of its own accord.

There is, of necessity, some 'telling' in the play. When read around the class, the script in itself will be sufficient. If staged, it's possible, as suggested by the script in Act 1, Scene 5, that behind or beside the actors proper, mime can be added. This technique could also be used in other places in the play, for example in Act 2, Scene 4, as the Captain describes the voodoo ceremony, and to dramatize Liliana's grief-stricken flight from the house, or the various deaths of the brothers.
(Be warned that this sort of staging needs impeccable timing.)

The actor who plays Sophie may find it difficult to speak in a gruff and aggressive enough voice to be convincing in Act 1, Scene 5. In this case, some offstage actor could provide the voice while Sophie mimes the doll's speech.

Lighting inventiveness will be needed for the final fire.

Costume and Props

Act 1

Scene 1

Daniel's nightshirt
Doll's house (to be used throughout Act 1)
Dog doll or toy
Several peg dolls (one, Mrs Golightly, is stick-thin and dressed exactly like Daniel's mother)
Old-fashioned lidded box in which all dolls fit (to be used throughout Act 1)
Bedside table, books
Chair
Bed with covers
Shawl
Old-fashioned doctor's bag
Fob watch
Stethoscope
Tongue compressor
Wardrobe
Dressing gown

Scene 2

Two sewing baskets
Unfinished garment that Mrs Marlow is making for Daniel
Dust sheet for doll's house

Scene 3

Lidded box with peg dolls

Scene 4

Painting easel and paints
Armchair
New frock for Sophie
New jacket for Daniel
Mrs Golightly doll

Scene 5

Double-headed, black-haired male peg doll in long skirts

Scene 6

Tray of tea things
Side table

Maid's apron
Letter in old-fashioned writing
Old-fashioned *Country Life*-style magazine
Needles and thread
Topknot-style loaf of bread
Long strips of material torn from a garment
The same, knotted into a hanging noose
Window bars
Stool

Act 2
Scene 1

Railway platform sign
Old-fashioned travel bag
Whistle
Four tiny lace-making tools in a small case
Handkerchief

Scene 2

Old-fashioned travel bag
Shawl
Rake
Six tombstones, one very small
Washing basket containing washing

Scene 3

Dining table and several chairs
Plates of food
Tray
Cutlery
Candelabra
Several paintings (no portraits)
Four tiny lace-making tools in a small case (from Act 2, Scene 1)

Scene 4

Bows
Arrows
Croquet mallet and balls
Cricket bats
Tennis racquets
Balls

Fishing rods
Old-fashioned board games, dice, etc.
Large account book and pen

Scene 5   Spade
Woven basket with a broken handle

Scene 6   · Seat (for Martha and Daniel)

Scene 7   Garden shears
Folded written note
Six tombstones, one very small (from Act 2, Scene 2)

Scene 8   Dining table laid with plates of food
Cutlery
Cloth napkins
Candelabra
Sharp knife
Tray

Scene 9   Desk with paper
Globe
Binoculars
Maps
Stuffed parrot
Witch doctor's mask
Short arrows in a jar
Cutlass or sword
Ship in a bottle
Large portrait of a man in naval uniform
Floor to ceiling drapes
Letter in old-fashioned writing

Act 3
Scene 1   Paper and a pen
Bed

Lace-making tool case (from Act 2, Scene 1)
Wall with sliding panel

Scene 2   Ivy-covered wall

Scene 3   Lace-making tool case (from Act 2, Scene 1)
Two tattered carpet bags
Old kettle
Two rusty saucepans
Rake
Spade
Old-fashioned box with dolls (from Act 1)
Fishing wire (for manikin)

Scene 4   Upturned wheelbarrow or half barrel

Character List

Liliana Cunningham	Comes from a refined family. Quiet and tense, she wears a white scalloped, high-necked blouse and stern black floor-length skirt. She gives off an aura of living with many secrets and even more fears.
Daniel Cunningham	Her son. Though close to bedridden when the story begins, he's frank, engaging and imaginative.
Dr Marlow	The local doctor. He's cheery, kind and generous.
Mrs Marlow	His wife. She's warm and motherly, though strict with her three daughters in the old-fashioned way of the time.
Cecilia Marlow	The eldest Marlow daughter. Pleasant and responsible.
Mary Marlow	The middle sister. Somewhat grave and always sensible.
Sophie Marlow	Is a couple of years younger than Daniel. She's cheerful, restless and irrepressible. Her parents and sisters think of her as 'untamed'.
Captain Severn	Is an imposing presence, with a shock of snow-white hair. Intensely mercurial by nature, one moment he's warm and friendly, the next fierce and terrifying. From time to time come flashes of sheer malevolence.
Thomas the Gardener	Is gruff and suspicious on the surface, but is essentially a loyal, kindly, middle-aged man.

Martha the Cook	She's also middle-aged and motherly but has a bitter streak born of her many griefs.
Gossips 1, 2 and 3	Gossiping neighbours of the Cunninghams
William, the Delivery Man	
Jane, the Marlow's Maid	
Two Nurses	
Train Guard	
Younger Country Woman	
Older Country Woman	
Carrier	
Villagers 1, 2, 3 and 4	

ACT 1

SCENE 1

*A small back bedroom in moonlight, with a narrow bed and bedside table piled with books. **Daniel**, in an old-fashioned nightshirt, sits cross-legged on the floor in front of a large doll's house. Beside him is a box of dolls and toy animals from which he's chosen a few to act out a story.*

Daniel

Come, Topper. You must know that it's your job to bark at robbers! How else can you protect poor Rubiana in her bed? You must wake Mrs Golightly. Come on. *[Imitates a dog]* Woof! Woof! Woof, woof! *[Breaks off, listening, afraid he's made too loud a noise, then carries on more softly]* Woof, woof! Good boy! You've done it! Here comes Mrs Golightly, down the stairs. She's cross enough at being woken, but she'll see the robbers off. *[He makes two male dolls run]* There they go, scuttling across the lawns into the woods. And Rubiana will be safe again. *[Yawns and stretches]* And I am tired too. The moon's across the sky. It must be nearly morning.

*Daniel puts all the dolls but one back in the box and closes the lid. Rising awkwardly, he gets back to bed unsteadily, and with the support of a chair back and the bedside table. He settles down and tugs the covers over. As he sleeps, the moonlight broadens to daylight and, to the side, as if outside, we see the **Gossips** whispering to one another.*

Gossip 1   There is a child in Hawthorn Cottage! Yes, truly! I saw him! He's pale and quiet – but he is a child!

Gossip 2   A child? In Hawthorn Cottage? With Mrs Cunningham? We never saw him arrive.

Gossip 3   No carriages have been around their door.

Gossip 2   Perhaps he has been hidden in the house for years!

Gossip 1   Oh, surely not!

Gossip 3   Whom should we tell? Whom should we tell?

Gossip 2   Why, Dr Marlow, of course!

Gossip 1   Yes, Dr Marlow!

*The **Gossips** hurry off.*

Liliana   *[Peeping in]* Ah, my dear boy's still sleeping. I'm glad. *[She tiptoes in and starts to tidy books and straighten bedclothes]* Stay there, my precious son, where you are safe. Safe in your bed. Safe here in your little back room, far from prying eyes.

***Liliana** picks up the stray doll and stares at it, puzzled, before looking back at **Daniel**. Shrugging, she puts it in the box.*

I bless each day that keeps you safe behind the tall hedges of this house, where I can still protect you. But still, I was a fool to listen to your pleading yesterday, and let you force me into helping you totter so slowly down the stairs into the garden. I know I heard a rustle in the hedge! I'll swear someone was peeping. *[She holds a hand to her heart]* Suppose they saw you sitting in the wicker chair? Suppose they gossip? Suppose the whisper gets about the town? *[In her panic, **Liliana** fails to notice **Daniel** is stirring]* Oh, if they find us out, how will I ever keep my poor son safe from his dread Uncle Se—

*A violent knocking on the door makes her break off in the middle of this name. **Daniel** wakes fully.*

| Daniel | What's that? Who's knocking? |

| Liliana | No one, my darling! *[Clearly panicking]* Maybe the butcher's boy. |

| Daniel | *[Scoffing]* He doesn't come this early. Take a look, Mama. |

*Nervously, **Liliana** crosses to the window but dare not look out in case she's seen. We hear murmurings outside.*

| Daniel | Throw up the sash, Mama. I can hear voices. |

| Liliana | *[Desperate]* I'm sure they're nothing to do with us, my sweet! |

| Daniel | But surely you should look. |

*Unwillingly, **Liliana** gathers courage and throws up the sash.*

| Gossip 1 | *[Off]* Mrs Cunningham? Mrs Cunningham? |

| Gossip 2 | *[Off]* Come to the door, please. |

| Liliana | *[Stepping back]* Merciful heavens! Who *are* these people? Who has found us out? |

| Daniel | Found us out? What can you mean, Mama? They call you by your name. Surely they are just neighbours! |

| Liliana | *[To self]* If only I could think so! |

| Gossip 1 | *[Off]* Mrs Cunningham! Please come to your door. There's something we must show you. |

| Gossip 3 | *[Off]* It is important. Please come down. |

Liliana *pulls in her head without speaking. At once the knocking on the door starts again, even more loudly.*

| Daniel | Mama, you'd better go. |

| Liliana | *[Clutching her heart]* Oh, I dare not! I dare not! |

| Daniel | They won't stop knocking. |

| Liliana | No. I fear they won't! Well, then, I must! |

Liliana gathers her shawl around her shoulders and hurries from the room. We hear footsteps and the unbolting of a door.

Liliana [*Stepping out*] What can you want with me? I cannot talk with you. I'm busy in my house.

Gossip 1 [*Taking one arm*] Please, Mrs Cunningham. You must step this way.

Gossip 3 [*Taking another arm*] We have something to show you.

Liliana Let go of my arm. I will not come. What's anything on the street to do with me? Stop pulling me away from my own door!

Gossip 1 Come, come! Compose yourself! Nobody wishes you the slightest harm.

Liliana [*Her voice getting fainter as she is pulled offstage*] No! Let me go! I must be with my child! What are you? You wear fine bonnets, but are you fiends from hell? Now let me go!

We hear a door slam and a bolt being drawn across.

Daniel My mother's gone! Those women have dragged her away. And someone's in our house. I hear doors opening! And I hear footsteps!

Heavy footsteps sound on the stairs.

Now they get closer! Up the stairs they come! What did my mother fear so much? What can be happening?

Daniel pulls the sheet up to under his eyes in fright and stares over it, mesmerized with fear, as the door slowly opens.

Dr Marlow [*Entering with his doctor's bag*] Well, here's a great surprise!

Daniel [*To self*] And one for me! Is this a doctor's bag he brings with him?

Dr Marlow It seems the whispering of all the ladies in the town is right. We have an invalid.

Daniel and Dr Marlow regard one another gravely.

Daniel [*Tremulously*] G-g-good morning to you, sir.

Dr Marlow	You have a voice, then. And good manners too. Have you a name as well?
Daniel	I'm Daniel Cunningham.
Dr Marlow	And I am Dr Marlow, come to examine you.
Daniel	Where have they taken my mother? Was all that commotion on the step simply a trick to get her out of the house, and you inside it?
Dr Marlow	*[Smiling]* I see you have wits as well. *[Sits on the bed and draws out a fob watch to check **Daniel**'s pulse]* And what's the name of your sickness, can you tell me?
Daniel	I do not know its name, only the weaknesses it leaves in me.
Dr Marlow	And what are those?
Daniel	My mother says my lungs are fearfully weak. She says my heart's not strong, it scarcely beats at all, and that my legs can barely carry me. She says I'm far too frail to lead a life like other boys.
Dr Marlow	And how long have you been this way.
Daniel	As long as I can remember.
Dr Marlow	As long as that? Then here's a mystery as well as a surprise!

*Opening his bag, **Dr Marlow** pulls out a stethoscope to listen to **Daniel**'s heart.*

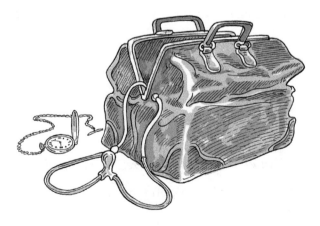

Dr Marlow	Breathe deeply, boy, if you please. Now cough. And cough again. Now open your mouth, if you will. *[He peers in **Daniel's** mouth, then reaches for his toes under the blankets]* And can you feel that?
Daniel	Certainly.
Dr Marlow	And this?
Daniel	Ouch, sir! Indeed I can.
Dr Marlow	*[Leaning back, clearly baffled]* So can you walk?
Daniel	*[Glancing to the door, to check his mother is not back to hear or see him]* Yes. I can walk.
Dr Marlow	Show me.
	Daniel slides his legs round and tentatively drops his weight on them. He is unsteady from lack of practice and muscle strength, but he can walk.
	[Astonished] Why, boy, there's absolutely nothing wrong with you!
Daniel	*[Incredulous]* Nothing wrong?
Dr Marlow	Nothing that hasn't sprung from lack of good fresh air and exercise.
Daniel	*[Confidently]* No, no. You're wrong, sir! *[Waving towards the window]* Look at the bright spring morning! If I were well, why would I be cooped up in this small room?
Dr Marlow	Yes, why indeed …? But I assure you that your lungs are strong, your heart beats manfully, and your legs are as wobbly as a newborn colt's only from lack of use.
Daniel	No, no! You have to be mistaken! My mother always says – no, she *insists* – that—
Dr Marlow	Hush, hush! I think perhaps we shouldn't talk about your mother – not till this little mystery is solved. *[Opening the wardrobe]* No outdoor clothes, I see. Is this your dressing gown? It will have to do. Come now. Wrap it around yourself, and we'll be gone.

Daniel	*[Shocked]* Gone? Gone *where*, sir? In all the time I can remember, I've never left this house.
Dr Marlow	All the more reason to go. Now, is there any comfort in this room that we can take along with us? *[Daniel looks blank]* What, nothing? Nothing in this room is precious to you?

Still in shock, **Daniel** *makes an effort to look round.*

Daniel	Precious? I cannot think! Well, yes. The doll's house, I suppose, has offered me my happiest hours.
Dr Marlow	This? *[Bending to look more closely]* Truly a labour of love! The finest of mansions, and most beautifully invented.
Daniel	It's not invented, sir. It's copied. My mother says it is the very image of her own childhood home, down to the last rosebud on the porch and the last coil of ivy.
Dr Marlow	No doubt it was the most idyllic place.
Daniel	She never said. She never speaks of anything in her past. *[Dr Marlow steadies Daniel as they move towards the door]* Sir, what will happen to me?
Dr Marlow	Be sure that Mrs Marlow and my daughters will welcome you into our house with open arms.
Daniel	*[Panicking]* But what about my mother?
Dr Marlow	You'll see her soon, boy. But first I must take time to ask her why she has kept you as a secret here, away from fresh air and wind and all the healthy pastimes a boy should share with others of his age.
Daniel	*[Wistfully]* It would be good to learn to throw a ball, like boys in books. And swim. And climb a tree.
Dr Marlow	Then let's be gone. Then you can start on your long journey out of this small room into the astonishing wide world.

Both look around one last time. **Dr Marlow** *propels* **Daniel** *out of the door. It closes behind them.*

SCENE 2

An old-fashioned drawing room. **Mrs Marlow, Cecilia** *and* **Mary** *are sewing.* **Daniel** *stands close to* **Mrs Marlow,** *who holds her handiwork against him to check the sizing.* **Sophie** *watches with excitement as the* **Delivery Man** *lays Daniel's box of dolls beside the shrouded doll's house he clearly carried in a minute before.*

Sophie	Oh, I can't wait! I cannot wait!
Delivery Man	There! *[Whipping off the dust sheet]* In all its glory! And it's a beauty. The finest doll's house that I've ever seen.
Sophie	I'll have such fun!
Mrs Marlow	Well, thank you, William. Dr Marlow will pay you. And no doubt Cook has some treat waiting for you in the kitchen.
Delivery Man	She usually does, Ma'am. This is the kindest household in the town.
	He touches his cap to her respectfully and leaves with his dust sheet.
Sophie	*[Diving into the box of dolls]* Oh, bliss! Oh, bliss!

Mary	Sophie! The doll's house belongs to Daniel, and he must choose if you can play with it.
Daniel	Of course Sophie must play with it, Mary! That's partly why your father sent for it – in order to distract her through these long days.
Sophie	How can a fever be so spiteful as to fall upon our town just as poor Daniel has begun to see the outside world for the first time!
Cecilia	*[To **Daniel**]* It must seem hard, to be cooped up again so soon.
Mary	Cecilia's right. You must have felt such disappointment when Father said that we must stay inside for two whole weeks in order to stay safe.
Cecilia	Still, there have been a host of first-time-evers for you, Daniel!
Mary	Yes. When you first came, we watched you stare at coloured window glass, and blink your eyes at chandeliers.
Sophie	You even claimed you'd never seen a sunset!
Daniel	Be fair to me, Sophie. I'd seen it rise a thousand times. It's just that my old bedroom faced east, not west.
Sophie	The horror of it! To be stuck indoors for your whole life. Not even let to roam within the house. Why, Cook will swear you'd never been inside a busy kitchen. She says you stared into her porridge pots as if the ploppings and the bubblings were quite as exciting as any volcano.
Daniel	Everything seemed so strange . . . And large. And colourful. And more real than in books.
Sophie	*[Merrily]* Especially your first live cow!
Daniel	*[Blushing]* It was so much more huge and weighty than I expected. And then, when you urged me to pat it—
Sophie	It raised a storm of dust. You were astonished.
Daniel	I was astonished by everything. I'd missed so much. It seemed to me that you three had had a real plum pudding of a life, stuffed with a million sights and sounds and feelings. And mine had been thin gruel.

Sophie	All of the things you'd never done! Sat on a wall. Stroked a pet rabbit. You'd never even thrown a pebble in a pond.
Daniel	*[Making a face]* Or had my clothes soaked through when someone's carriage wheel spun through a puddle.
Mrs Marlow	You will have clothes enough, when we have finished our stitching.
Daniel	You are so kind to me. So I'll be kind to Sophie, and tell her that the doll's house is hers through these long weeks we have to stay inside.
Sophie	Then I'm in heaven!
	As **Sophie** *chooses dolls,* **Dr Marlow** *enters quietly.*
	You'll be the mother doll. And you're the father. *[She turns]* Daniel, I meant to ask you. Do *you* have a father?
Mary	Sophie! Perhaps Daniel doesn't choose to talk about his family.
Mrs Marlow	Yes, Sophie. If Daniel would prefer to keep his past life private, we must let him be.
Daniel	No, no. I have no secrets from such friends as you. I'm not so foolish as to think I never had a father. And yet my mother never happily mentioned him. Though once, when I pestered her into a flurry, she told me that he had gone off to Glory just before my birth.
Sophie	*[Baffled]* Gone off to Glory?
Cecilia	*[Whispering]* That means he died.
Sophie	Oh! Well, have you no relatives? No aunts or uncles? No cousins?
Daniel	None that I heard of – except that once, as I woke, I'm sure I heard my mother whispering an uncle's name – well, half a name. I heard her muttering to herself about an 'Uncle Se—' Then she broke off.
Sophie	So you could have an Uncle Septimus. Or Seth. Or Sebastian. Or—

Dr Marlow	Enough! Or our poor Daniel will find himself knee-deep in uncles.
Sophie	But visitors? Surely your mother must have had friends and visitors! Surely the two of you could not have lived entirely hidden and alone.
Daniel	Indeed we did. I think my mother is a quiet woman.
Sophie	*[Innocently]* You're generous indeed! For all the rest of the town says that your mother is insane.
Mrs Marlow	Sophie! For shame!

Mrs Marlow, Cecilia and Mary drop their sewing to usher Sophie hastily from the room.

Sophie	*[Defending herself]* But why else should Mrs Cunningham have taken it upon herself to keep her own son locked in a dull dark room?
Cecilia	Sophie!
Mary	How could you? Shocking words! Now you are in disgrace!

The door shuts behind them, leaving Dr Marlow staring at Daniel, who is fighting tears.

• •

SCENE 3

Dr Marlow steps forward to put an arm round Daniel's shoulder.

Dr Marlow	What Sophie said must pain you horribly. Be sure I will be strict with my foolish daughter on this matter.
Daniel	No, no. She said it in all innocence, not out of spite. I can forgive her easily and so must you.
Dr Marlow	*[Steps back to study Daniel]* Daniel, I will admit that sometimes you puzzle me greatly.
Daniel	Puzzle you, sir? But how?
Dr Marlow	Something about your manner. And your understanding. Think. All these years you've been locked away from all companionship—

Daniel	Except that of my mother.
Dr Marlow	True. Yet she seems to have shown herself, even to you, as silent and secretive.
Daniel	She did not chatter, no. And she was not prepared to tell me anything about her past – or mine.
Dr Marlow	And yet, here in our noisy and disordered household, you seem to fit in well. *[Pause]* Perhaps *too* well?
Daniel	*Too* well?
Dr Marlow	Everything's new to you. Wind. Weather. Every animal you stroke or pass. I've seen your mouth drop open at such a simple sight as bread dough rising in a bowl. Everything in the world is new to you, Daniel. Everything! Except for people.
Daniel	People?
Dr Marlow	Listen, my boy. If you'd met nobody, where did you learn, right from the start, to address a man like myself as 'Sir' and my dear wife as 'Madam' or 'Mrs Marlow'? Why are you never put out by Sophie's teasing for your attention? You recognize when Mary is irritated, or Cecilia tired. You hear that snippet of cruel gossip about your mother, and know the words at once for what they are – sheer thoughtlessness, not spite. In short, Daniel, stuck in that room with only your sad mother for company, how did you ever learn to be so comfortable in a family?
Daniel	From books, perhaps? Reading can teach you to understand the world and how it works.
Dr Marlow	No, that won't serve. You no doubt read of cows in books, but you were still astonished to see something so huge and overpowering as the real thing. And people are far more complex than cows. No, there is something in the sheer ease of how, from the very start, you have known what to do and what to say, and how to fit in with others . . .

Daniel	Oh, that! Why, that is nothing. I've always lived that sort of life. Only I lived it at night, in secret on the floor, in moonlight.
Dr Marlow	The floor? In moonlight? How?
Daniel	*[Pointing]* There, sir! I lived my real life there! In and around the doll's house! *[He picks dolls out of the box]* See, here's my boy Hal – though sometimes he's a prince, but always good and true. Here's thin, stiff Mrs Golightly! She is a stern one! Here's smiling Rubiana. The times Hal's rescued her – and she has rescued him. All with the help of Topper. Here's my dog, Topper. He's a brave sort. And all the others in the box. Dolls who can pass for sturdy sailors one day and evil pirates the next, depending on my story.
Dr Marlow	You learned to live among real people simply from your imagination and this set of dolls?
Daniel	So it would seem.
Dr Marlow	I am astonished!
Daniel	*[Teasing]* And so it seems my mother did not do so bad a job of raising me, even alone.
Dr Marlow	Indeed, it seems she did not.
Daniel	And so, when may I see her?
Dr Marlow	*[Evasively]* Ah, now. The fever . . .
Daniel	But even before the fever, each time I asked, you hummed and hawed and found some reason why I should not visit her. But she's my mother! And I miss her terribly. I have no doubt she wants to see me! Unless, what the townspeople say is true . . .
Dr Marlow	It's true your mother's not herself at present . . .
Daniel	But she loves me! And I love her, and long to see her. When can I visit her? When? If I don't go, she will begin to think I have abandoned her.
Dr Marlow	I promise you, as soon as I think she will be better for a visit from you, I will arrange it.

Daniel	She *cannot* be so crazed she wouldn't be the better for seeing me.
Dr Marlow	Her mind is hectic, Daniel. It hovers on a knife-edge. You must be patient.
Daniel	Just till the fever's gone from the town?
Dr Marlow	If I can persuade myself that seeing you won't trouble your mother more, then yes, when the fever's gone. And now, until that day, you'll try to be a happy and untroubled boy?
Daniel	I'll try.
Dr Marlow	And perhaps, in the meantime, you and your dolls will even manage to teach young Sophie manners as fine as your own.
Daniel	Perhaps. Though even I can see that that's a task as hard as many of Hal's most demanding adventures.

Dr Marlow and Daniel share a smile and a hug.

• •

SCENE 4

The drawing room. Mary sits stitching as Cecilia sketches a portrait of her. Sophie is in a different frock and Daniel a new jacket to indicate a different day. The two of them are sprawled in front of the doll's house, playing a merry game.

Sophie	So then the guard dog barks some more. Woof! Woof! And then he growls. Growwwwwl!
Daniel	Pathetic, Sophie! You've played with Topper now for two whole weeks, and still the only growl that you can manage couldn't scare a duck.
Sophie	You do the growling then.
Daniel	How can I growl *and* play the butcher's boy? I know. I'll get Hal here to chuck a sausage from the package he's delivering. The dog will stop his growling.
Sophie	And start to gulp instead. [*To Mary's horror, and Daniel and Cecilia's amusement, Sophie makes loud gulping noises*]

27

Mary	Sophie! For shame! Where are your manners?
Sophie	I think that, for a dog, my manners are quite excellent. The very best.
Daniel	They're certainly better than your growls! Sophie, the day you learn to throw any voice but your own will be a day of wonders!
Sophie	Am I so bad at imitation? Then I must send for someone who'll be strict with you, and tell you not to criticize your fond companion in play. *[She reaches for the stick-thin doll, Mrs Golightly]* There! Please scold him for his rudeness, Mrs Cunningham.
Daniel	*[Startled]* Mrs *Cunningham?*
Mary	*[Shocked]* Sophie!
Cecilia	Sophie?
Sophie	*[Realizing her mistake]* Oh, Daniel! Forgive me! I didn't mean to use your mother's name. I know the doll is called Mrs Golightly. It was a slip of the tongue. *[**Sophie** holds up the doll, who looks, and is dressed, exactly like **Liliana** Cunningham]* But Cecilia and I did see your mother paying the butcher's boy on the step one morning. And you'll admit this doll's her spitting image.
Daniel	*[Disturbed]* I'd never realized.
Mary	*[Kindly]* Nor would you, Daniel. You didn't see the women of the town. How would you know they don't *all* wear prim, snow-white blouses and black skirts reaching to the ground when they go off on errands.
Sophie	And it is not so strange. After all, if the doll's house was made to look so exactly like your family's old house that Father asked Cecilia to paint a portrait of it—
Cecilia	*[Whispers]* Hush, Sophie! That was a secret!
Sophie	*[Covering her mouth]* Oh, I had forgot! I'll say no more about that! *[She turns back to **Daniel**]* Well, why should the dolls inside it not look like members of the family?

Cecilia	Yes, Daniel. Perhaps Mrs Golightly was modelled on your grandmother, and over the years your mother has grown to look like her.
Daniel	*[Inspecting the doll]* There is a likeness. That can't be denied. *[He turns to **Sophie**]* Then I forgive you for confusing this stick-thin and unhappy creature with my own mother. And when she's well again, I will make sure to stuff the larder in Hawthorn Cottage with every manner of food to fatten her, so you will never make the mistake again.
Sophie	*[Surprised]* But did you not know? You won't be going back to Hawthorn Cottage. Your house is taken.
	Mary and **Cecilia** hold their breath.
Daniel	*[Bemused]* Taken? How, 'taken'?
	Mary hurries from the room to fetch **Mrs Marlow**.
Sophie	It's let again. It has been rented out to a new family. And Mrs Parker says there are four children, one for each year of the marriage.
Cecilia	Hush, Sophie. Enough!
Sophie	But it is true. And Mrs Parker swears that she has already seen the whole tribe tumbling about the garden.
Mrs Marlow	*[Hurrying in]* Sophie!
	Mary and **Cecilia** usher **Sophie** from the room. **Mrs Marlow** stays.
Daniel	How can that house belong to others now? It is my *home!*
Mrs Marlow	*[Sitting in the armchair and reaching out for him]* Not if your mother has failed to pay the quarter's rent, my dear.
Daniel	But I thought I'd live there forever. I thought that I was only staying here until my mother was well again, and then— And then we'd— And then together, she and I would—

*Daniel bursts into sobs. He throws himself at **Mrs Marlow**'s feet. He hugs her knees. She strokes his hair. Silently **Dr Marlow** enters and stands watching as **Daniel**'s shoulders heave with grief.*

• •

*The drawing room, a short while later. **Sophie** is playing alone. She does not notice as **Daniel** appears in the doorway.*

Sophie

[To a doll] Now I must quickly arrange for your escape, or you'll swing on the scaffold, and I could not bear to think of that.

Daniel

Too harsh a fate for my soft-hearted Sophie to offer anyone?

Sophie

Daniel! You're back! I am so sorry! What I said was stupid and thoughtless! You see I am so happy to have you with us here, it's easy to forget you might have had some other hopes and plans.

Daniel

Forget all that. My tears have dried. Come, let's get on with rescuing your pirate before the lunch bell rings.

Sophie

I'll have him fight his way upstairs. One, two! One, two! Slash, slash! Yes! Push them all down the stairs and up you go, into the attic.

Daniel

There to be trapped forever.

Sophie

No, no. He's leaving through the sliding panel.

Daniel

What sliding panel?

Sophie

The one I found while you were with Mama.

Daniel

What, in my doll's house?

Sophie

Yes. Here.

*Daniel kneels to watch as **Sophie** moves something in an attic room of the doll's house.*

Daniel

I never saw that. I never realized.

Sophie

You need small fingers.

Daniel

I had small fingers once. Look! Now your pirate can get up on to the roof—

Sophie	And so escape down the strong coils of ivy.
Daniel	Like Jack on his beanstalk!
Sophie	But he has left a glorious mess behind him. I must put that to rights. And see? Here's a tiny pin, loose on the window seat. I'll push it back. *[Withdraws her hand to suck a finger]* Ouch! That's another nail come up.
Daniel	Leave it to me!
Sophie	No. I'll just prise them out and— Oh! Oh, no! Daniel, I'm sorry. I've sprung the pins along the window seat. *[Peering]* And there is something inside.

Sophie holds up a thin carved boy doll in long skirts.

Daniel	Another doll? Hidden inside the doll's house all these years?
Sophie	Yes. A cheeky young boy. Lying inside the window seat for all the world as if he were already in his coffin! *[Sophie flips the doll over]* And look! Flip the doll over and he's grown into a man.
Daniel	Two dolls in one? I only wish I'd known!
Sophie	He would have been a grand addition to your little cast when you played all alone.
Daniel	He will be now, while we make stories together.
Sophie	*[In the gruffest, most aggressive voice]* I'll be no plaything in *your* stories. No, not I! I'll turn each tale whichever way I want!

Sophie throws down the double-headed doll as if it has scorched her, then claps a hand over her mouth as if both startled and horrified by what has burst out of it.

Daniel	*[Startled]* Sophie! I'd no idea that you could ape such a rough voice.
Sophie	*[Scared]* Neither had I. *[She stares uneasily at the new doll]*
Daniel	Come, Sophie! It's a stick of wood. On with the game.

Sophie	*[Nervously,* **Sophie** *picks up the doll and inspects it]* Oh, Daniel! I threw it down too hard. I've scratched his face.
	Sophie *shows* **Daniel***.*
Daniel	*[Hoping to comfort]* No matter, Sophie. See? His hair falls over his fresh scar. And it will make him seem a better enemy when he is called to play that part.
Sophie	*[In the same gruff voice]* A part I will play well! *[***Sophie*** looks horrified. The doll shakes violently in her hand]* Yes, set *me* to catch your precious pirate. I'll cut him into tatters and seize his treasures for myself.
	Sophie *stares wildly round as if searching for the source of the voice.*
Daniel	Strange . . . *[Trying to convince himself]* But when one plays at pirates . . . *[To Sophie]* Well, on with the story.
Sophie	*[In the gruff voice]* Yes! On with the story! My knives are razor sharp! I cannot wait to make good use of them!
	Horrified, **Sophie** *throws down the doll.*
Daniel	Sophie?
Sophie	*[In her own voice]* No! I won't play! No, not today!
	Sophie *snatches up the doll, thrusts him inside the doll box and slams down the lid.*
Daniel	*[Sharing her great unease]* Yes, put the dolls away. We'll play another morning.
	They gather a few strewn dolls. But neither wants to lift the doll box lid again, and when they throw in the last dolls they slam the lid back down fast, as if they feared something that lay inside.

• •

SCENE 6

Jane the maid comes in with a tea tray as **Sophie** *and* **Daniel** *scramble to their feet. She starts to lay things out on a side table as* **Mrs Marlow** *and* **Cecilia** *follow her in.* **Mrs Marlow** *is waving a handwritten letter and* **Cecilia** *has an old-fashioned magazine.*

Mrs Marlow	Daniel, there's news! It seems you have an uncle living.
Daniel	An uncle? How did you find me an uncle?
Mrs Marlow	Ah, we are cleverer than you think! You told the doctor that the doll's house was the very image of your mother's home. And so he asked Cecilia to paint a portrait of it.
Sophie	The secret I let out!
Daniel	I had forgotten that you mentioned it.
Mrs Marlow	We put an advertisement in this magazine.
Cecilia	*[Opening it proudly]* Along with this copy of my painting.

Mrs Marlow	And we have received a reply. From someone who claims your mother was his precious sister who ran away from home when she was little more than seventeen, and has been vanished since.
Daniel	I have an uncle? A real uncle? Living all this time?

Mrs Marlow	He wants to see you. *[Tapping the letter]* He says here that he cannot wait to have you come to visit him at High Gates.
Daniel	High Gates?
Mrs Marlow	It is the name of the house. The *real* house.
Daniel	But I must ask my mother! As soon as the fever's gone from her side of the town as well as ours—
Jane	The fever? Why that's been gone from everywhere around the town for more than a week now.
Mrs Marlow	Hush, Jane!

Realizing her mistake, **Jane** *scurries out, past* **Dr Marlow** *who is hurrying in, clearly distressed.*

Daniel	More than a week? But then, why did the doctor say it lingered round the hospital? And why has he not taken me to see my mother? *[To* **Dr Marlow***]* You promised me! You know you promised me. 'Wait till the fever's gone' you told me. Why have you kept me from her even longer than you might?
Dr Marlow	*[Nervously]* Daniel, your mother was much changed. She has been very ill.
Daniel	Much changed? And very ill? *[Angrily]* Perhaps she would have been a good deal better if your kindness had stretched to letting me visit her!
Dr Marlow	You would not have recognized her.

As the scene proceeds, the lighting changes and we see on a different part of the stage, possibly only in silhouette, a lunatic asylum cell. Window bars, or their shadows, are visible. **Liliana** *and the* **Nurses** *are silently acting out what* **Dr Marlow** *goes on to describe.*

You think of your mother as the gentle soul who sat beside your bed. But when we took her to the hospital she became frantic. She could not be comforted, and begged to be set free so she could lock you up again, safe from some old, old evil that was threatening you. We could not keep her safe without firm

34

locks. And in her tiny cell she tore her dress and stitched and crocheted in a fury. At times she paced and paced, weeping and muttering about a host of dreadful deaths. Each day, the nurses said, the story and the victim's name had changed. But still she could not be persuaded these deaths were mere illusions – the grim imaginings of a frenzied mind.

Daniel   My mother . . . frantic? Frenzied?

*We see **Liliana** hiding from the **Nurses** the length of braiding she has torn from her clothing and been stitching so frantically.*

Dr Marlow   Oh, she was in a storm of misery and rage. She hurled her bread upon the floor. She screeched and spat, and flew at the nurses' faces with her fingernails, cursing us all.

Daniel   *Cursed* you? My *mother*?

Dr Marlow   She acted like a woman unhinged. It reached the stage where nurses scarcely dared go in. At night she never slept – just prayed and howled.

Daniel   My mother *howled*?

Dr Marlow   The nurses said it was like listening to a wolf bay at the moon. Now do you see why I have kept you from her? I blessed the fever when it came, because it gave me one more firm excuse to keep a boy from seeing his mother in such a wild and desperate state.

Daniel   Wild? Desperate? No I can't bear this! Don't say any more!

Dr Marlow   *[Softly]* But there is more, Daniel. And it is worse. For your dear mother. And for you.

Daniel   How, 'worse'? What could be worse?

Dr Marlow   Oh, Daniel! When I visited today, there was a flurry in a nearby cell. Some torn skin. Simply a matter of a few stitches. But I did call for aid. So Matron called the nurse out of your mother's cell, thinking she'd be away for only a minute or two.

*Left alone, **Liliana** pulls out the braided noose she's hidden, picks up a stool and leaves the stage in the direction of the window bars.*

And while the nurse and I were busy just two doors away along the corridor, your mother climbed upon a stool, and with a noose she'd used her skills to make—

A flash. A clap of thunder.

Your mother hanged herself!

Darkness

ACT 2

• •

SCENE 1

The railway station. Sounds of steam hissing, voices, etc. A forlorn
Daniel *carries a carpet bag.*

Dr Marlow   So you'll be brave?

Daniel   I have no choice, it seems. You say that I must go.

Dr Marlow   This Captain Severn is your blood family. And he gave me as
little choice as I give you.

Daniel   Still – to go over a hundred miles! By train. Alone! To someone
I have never met, nor even heard of till a week ago. And
someone whom my mother was clearly never keen for me to
know.

Dr Marlow   *[Obviously anxious]* That was a worry, certainly. *[Cheering]* But,
Daniel, whatever happens, there will always be a home waiting
for you here.

Daniel   You promise me?

Dr Marlow   I promise.

A whistle sounds.

Train Guard   Now climb aboard, young sir, or we shall leave without you.

Dr Marlow   Wait! Your mother left you no inheritance. And you insist the
doll's house must stay here with Sophie – at least till your
future's settled. Still, I've a token of your past for you to take
along with you.

Dr Marlow fishes in his pocket and brings out a tiny ivory case.

Daniel   My mother's lace-making tools!

Daniel unscrews the top and tips them into his hand.

Dr Marlow   So delicate. Like four pretty matchsticks. They're for
remembrance.

Daniel	She is not someone I would ever forget. And, if I speak the truth, the only reason I obey you in this matter, and step on this train, is that I'm curious to find out more about her early life, and why she kept me so – so—
Dr Marlow	Secluded?
Daniel	*[Angrily]* Entombed!

The whistle blows again. **Daniel** *leaves to join the train. We hear it chug away, and watch* **Dr Marlow** *wave his handkerchief, then turn away to wipe his eyes.*

Dr Marlow	*[Softly]* Be brave, my boy. Be brave.

· ·

SCENE 2

A wooded path, at twilight. A tired **Daniel**, *carrying his bag, meets* **two Country Women** *coming the other way.*

Daniel	Excuse me, ladies. May I beg some help. I'm trying to find High Gates.
Older Woman	*[Clutching her shawl in fright]* High Gates?
Younger Woman	Young man, you would do better to beg our help to find the path *away* from such a place.
Daniel	I beg your pardon?
Younger Woman	No matter! We must be gone. *[She points behind her]* If you must find High Gates, look for the two stone eagles.
Older Woman	But take care. Take care!

The **two Country Women** *hurry off.* **Daniel** *goes further along the path.*

Daniel	Stone eagles? Of course! There! There on the gateposts. How grim and threatening they look. So real they seem to watch my every step. *[Nervously]* Now it grows cold and dark. Those women spoke so strangely of the place. My uncle cannot care for me as much as he declares. His promises to meet me from the train were worthless. If this were not my only chance to

see my mother's childhood home I would turn back right now
and—

Thomas, *carrying home his rake, steps out of the shadows and notices* ***Daniel.***

Thomas Young man, we'll have no trespassing by strangers here. *[Peering more closely]* My God! It cannot be! But he's the very like . . .

Daniel The very like?

Thomas No, I'll not say a word. Except I never thought to see those eyes again. *[He hurries off]* No, never. Never.

Daniel Are my eyes so like my mother's? And must I find my own way through this wilderness? What's this? A beech hedge grown so high my mother must have known the place. The little gate's unlocked. The path winds round as if it were a maze. Come on, moon! Play your part. I want to see what's in this little clearing, so tucked away out of sight. Oh! *[Nervously]* Are they tombstones? *[In growing horror]* All of them? So many graves so near one house? *[He shivers violently]* Oh, horrors! This is no place to be!

Daniel *runs back, out of the gate and collides with* ***Martha,*** *who is carrying a washing basket. The washing spills.*

Oh! I beg your pardon!

*Daniel stoops to help gather the spilled washing. As he bends close to **Martha**'s face, she sees his.*

Martha   Oh, no! Oh, it's too much! The very image! My poor heart! Oh, my poor heart!

*Abandoning the basket, **Martha** hurries off.*

Daniel   *[Gathering the washing]* Now here's a fine new home, where everyone who sees me treats me like a ghost from some grim past. I've such a mind to turn my steps away. Except that clearly there are secrets here, and if I'm ever to understand why my dear mother kept me locked away, I must be braver than this.

*Determinedly, **Daniel** goes the way **Martha** went. Seeing the house, he stops dead.*

It is the doll's house! To the very life! Am I back in my little room? Have all the storms and confusions of the last few weeks been nothing but a dream?

***Captain Severn** steps into view.*

Captain Severn   Who's this? Who's this? *[Peering into the dark]* Why, is it my nephew, Daniel? Is it, at last? *[Striding to greet him]* So you have found our small apology for a station. I knew you would! Come, come! Give me your bag!

Daniel   Truly, it holds so little . . .

Captain Severn   *[Merrily]* Then even a feeble fellow like myself can prise it from your hand.

Daniel   *[Staring at the house]* This is a splendid place!

Captain Severn   Splendid indeed! I'll put you in the highest attic room, so you can see over the countryside as far as Farley Down. But right now, you must come inside and dine with me. *[Calling]* Martha, our young man's here! And no doubt like all others of his age, he has a wolf in his belly! *[Wagging a finger at **Daniel**]* You must be on your guard. Martha will feed you so well you'll soon peer in a looking glass and think yourself a barrel! Oh, I am glad to see you. You'll be so happy here. Though I can't find you company of your own age, there'll still be plenty to do. Why, I can teach you how to hunt and fish!

*He steers **Daniel** towards the house.*

Yes, yes! Come in to my house. I could not be more pleased to see you. Up until now I have been rattling around it all alone, like a dead beetle shaken in a bottle!

*Somewhat disturbed at the image, **Daniel** goes ahead.*

[*Softly to self, with menace*] Or perhaps, more like a spider in his web. Just waiting, merely waiting, for you to come . . .

● ●

SCENE 3

*A drab, neglected dining room that has clearly seen better times. Darker rectangular marks on the wallpaper show where at least five portraits must have been removed. One end of the long table is set for two, and most of the supper is already in place. **Daniel** wanders in alone.*

Daniel   [*Staring about*] This house is so alike – and yet so different. My doll's house is a bright and cheerful place. Yet this, its very twin, feels steeped in gloom – sunk in unhappiness. And in my doll's house there are portraits on every wall. Perhaps my uncle doesn't choose to be reminded of what a lonely life he's led. Or perhaps he's moved the paintings of the ones he loved to his own room, so they'll be closer to his memory.

*We hear footsteps. **Daniel** moves to his seat at the table as **Captain Severn** strides in, followed by **Martha** carrying in the last of the food.*

Captain Severn   Ah, here's the boy! Prompt for his dinner! See, Martha? His poor dear mother must have raised him well.

__Martha__ sets down the food and leaves, her head lowered.

Daniel   Good evening, sir.

Captain Severn   And to you, sir! [*Beaming*] And now the two of us must get to know one another.

41

*A significant silence as **Captain Severn**'s smile vanishes entirely. He studies **Daniel**, who becomes more and more uncomfortable.*

Captain Severn   *[Aggressively]* So, Daniel. Tell how my sister Liliana fared, once she had fled from all who trusted and loved her.

Daniel   *[To self]* Oh, here's a fighting start! *[To **Captain Severn**]* As far back as I can remember, the two of us lived quietly together.

Captain Severn   Liliana? Quiet? Now there's a fine surprise for those of us who knew her as a child!

Daniel   *[To self]* And what my uncle says is even more of a surprise to me!

Captain Severn   Quiet, you say? So did your mother mingle with the townsfolk? No ladies who became her warmest friends? No handsome men who hoped to win her widow's heart and call you son and heir?

Daniel   No, sir.

Captain Severn   You can be *sure*?

Daniel   We lived in one another's pockets. So I am sure.

Captain Severn   And did she ever speak about this house? What did she say of me?

Daniel   She never spoke of you.

Captain Severn   What, *never*? Not a *word*?

Daniel   No, not a word.

Captain Severn   Not the least mention of all the years she lived here?

Daniel   No, not to me.

Captain Severn   Well, well. Not a single word. *[As if he has forgotten **Daniel**'s presence]* Clearly there's more than one way in the world to rid oneself of an unwanted life . . . *[He snaps back to the present]* And tell me, what did your mother think most precious in this little house of hers?

Daniel	Apart from me?
Captain Severn	*[Dismissively]* Yes, yes! Apart from you.
Daniel	I'm sure that I don't know. The house did not belong to us. Nor did the silver or the furniture. We had so few things of our own. But I will tell you what's most precious to me. *[Pulls out the lace-making tool case]* It is a token of my mother's sad, short life.

Martha has stepped in silently behind Captain Severn to clear the plates. At the sight of the tool case, she freezes, clearly moved. Captain Severn, meanwhile, makes a dismissive gesture.

Captain Severn	I have no interest in your sentimental trinkets! Was there a doll's house?
Daniel	*[Quietly furious]* A doll's house?
Captain Severn	*[Rapping the table]* Yes! Dolls! Dolls that your mother stole from this house!
Daniel	*[Icily]* I'm sure my mother only ever took away from any house things that she thought her own.
Captain Severn	So you have seen no doll's house and no dolls?
Daniel	*[Blandly]* I had no sisters, sir.
Captain Severn	Nor any brothers, either, so it seems. *[Menacingly to self]* So less for me to do, and quicker work . . . *[He pulls himself together]* No, no! Your first night in this place! I mustn't grill you about my poor dear sister and her pitiful life. We'll talk more cheerfully of all the things that High Gates has to offer. The river and the rides. The badgers' sett. The courtyard and shrubberies. The Devil Walks.
Daniel	The Devil Walks?
Captain Severn	That's where the gentlemen of the house strode off to curse and swear. *[Laughing uproariously]* It doesn't take a lot to make the ladies blush! And so their menfolk strode to the Devil Walks to spill their fury. You know the kind of thing: *[Imitates]* 'The devil take him! 'Blast that man into hell! A curse on him and every last one of his family!' No one would be distressed by outbursts hidden away behind such high beech hedges.

Daniel	Behind beech hedges? Do you mean that sad, sad circle of graves? Well, then, I have already found the place!
Captain Severn	*[Suddenly icy]* Really? I see that you have lost no time in prowling about the grounds.
Daniel	Prowling? If it's a place you would prefer me not to go . . .
Captain Severn	A place I would prefer you not to go? No, no! *[Grinning malevolently]* The very opposite! Daniel, I tell you honestly, I cannot wait to see you in the Devil Walks. Oh, no. I cannot wait . . .

• •

SCENE 4

The following morning, on the veranda. It's scattered with pastimes carried from some dusty cupboard: bows, arrows, croquet mallets, cricket bats, tennis racquets, balls, fishing rods, an old bagatelle board game, etc. **Daniel** *is sorting through them.* **Captain Severn** *sits idly studying his estate account book.*

Captain Severn	*[Muttering]* . . . What, five more barrels? Not at that pretty price! This house eats money for breakfast and dinner both.
Daniel	This is a treasure trove! I've never seen so many fine amusements in my life!
Captain Severn	I only wish that I could stay to introduce you to each one. It's far too fine a day for paying bills and ordering supplies. Later we'll go to the woods. I'll show you where your mother cut her knee jumping from some high branch, and bled like a stuck pig. And the old hollow oak, where she played 'Squirrels' all day.
Daniel	*[Baffled]* She sounds a merry soul.
Captain Severn	She was, she was. *[He picks up the rod]* I'll show you the river, too, and teach you how to fish! *[Pointing]* We'll sit together on that wide fallen cedar where the lightning struck.
Daniel	It must have been a flash to wonder at, to fetch down such a tree. You didn't see it happen?
Captain Severn	No, no. By then I had gone off to sea.

44

Daniel	And had excitements and adventures?
Captain Severn	Little else! Why, boy, you haven't run till you've outraced a poisoned dart.
Daniel	I would be dead from fear alone.
Captain Severn	Better to save your worries for stranger terrors. Why, there are lands where, after nightfall, drums pound. There's eerie singing. And there are squawking chickens killed for sacrifice and altars sticky with blood. And in the darkness you see men and women with fearsome masks. They hold small figures crudely carved from roots, or fashioned out of clay, and they call up strange powers with their chanted spells.
Daniel	What sort of spells?
Captain Severn	Spells of all kinds. Spells to bring love, or end it. Spells to make people sicken or die. Spells of revenge.
Daniel	When Mrs Marlow took me into church to be baptized, the vicar said that, though the devil walks, he'll make no headway if he is not invited in.
Captain Severn	Your kindly, innocent vicar may hope he's right. But he has clearly never come across the powers of voodoo.
Daniel	Voodoo?
Captain Severn	It works by stealth. You make a little wooden doll and name it for the one you have in mind. You cast your spell. And after that, the doll and who it was you made it for are intertwined till death. If you torment the doll, your enemy will writhe in misery. Shower favours on it and your friend will thrive.
Daniel	Beyond imagining! And do you miss this life of such excitement?
Captain Severn	No, no. Seafaring is a fine and useful past. But I am set on quite a different future.
Daniel	Here?
Captain Severn	[Scoffing] Here? In *this* backwater? Along with one ancient sulking crone of a housekeeper whose wits have twisted out

of shape from grief, and a grim gardener who scowls at me each time I dare to step from my own house? Lord, I've a finer destiny mapped out than that! I'll soon be gone.

Daniel	Gone?
Captain Severn	Yes. In as little time as it can take for one thing to be found, and yet another – *[Looking meaningfully at **Daniel** and snapping out the last word]* – lost! *[He glowers. Then suddenly his mood changes. Chuckling, he grasps his account book]* Now I'm away, to polish off my dry and miserable calculations. You can stay here, or go exploring, as you choose.

***Captain Severn** goes into the house, whistling cheerfully, as **Daniel** stares after him.*

Daniel	*[Anxiously]* Why do my uncle's moods spin on a sixpence? He stared at me in such a strange way! What did he mean, 'and yet another lost'?

• •

SCENE 5

*As **Daniel** stands thinking, **Thomas** moves into view, busy with his spade. **Martha** comes in, carrying a woven basket with a broken handle.*

Martha	Spare me a moment, Thomas. I'd take an hour to make this broken handle worse. You'll fix it in an instant.
Thomas	Give it to me.

***Thomas** starts to fix the handle back in place. **Daniel** comes close.*

Daniel	You're Thomas. You're the gardener I met last night.
Thomas	You need no introduction of your own.
Martha	*[To **Daniel**]* I hope you slept well.
Daniel	I should have, Martha, after your splendid supper. And I was tired enough. And yet I tossed and turned. The damp stains on the walls became disfigured faces. The people in my dreams opened their mouths to speak and I saw fangs. My night seemed plagued by goblins, and I felt some ancient evil was pursuing me.

Martha and Thomas exchange furtive glances.

I woke and thought, 'I must be gone from here at once!' And yet – And yet—

Martha	And yet—?
Daniel	I must know more about my mother! I want to see her childhood haunts.
Thomas	An easy enough task, since there's no barn or tree for miles around that wasn't one of them.
Martha	Yes. Liliana was a lively child.
Thomas	Talkative. Merry.
Martha	*[Fondly]* But with a fiery temper when she was crossed.
Thomas	Ah, Martha. The times you scolded her for hiding in trees, and jumping across streams.

Daniel moves away from them.

Daniel	Hiding in trees and jumping across streams? Not like the mother I knew! Here is a mystery. Can one person truly be two? For now I see the glorious surroundings in which my mother spent her own early life – these woods and fields, that river, lawns that burst with daisies, clean breezes and a hundred bright amusements – I cannot help but feel she did me terrible wrong to keep me locked away. How can I love her memory the way I would, when everywhere I look shows me she knew what childhood happiness should be? And yet, to me, she offered only a small back room and one long lie. And that was cruel. So cruel! No, no. The Liliana they speak of cannot have been my mother. These two old folk must be mistaken somehow.

Daniel has a sudden idea and turns back to Martha and Thomas.

Is there no portrait of my mother as a child?

Martha	You've seen yourself, the portraits are long gone. Your uncle burned them all – except his own.

Daniel	Burned them? But why?
Martha	Conscience, perhaps? *[She glances round as if to check the Captain is not in sight]* It's my belief that even a painted eye can look reproachful.
Thomas	*[Bitterly]* Martha is right. You will be wasting your time looking for portraits of Liliana – or any of her brothers.
Daniel	*Brothers?* Not just the *one?* *[Aside]* How many secrets has she kept from me!
Martha	*[Astonished]* You didn't know about her brothers? And their sad deaths?
Daniel	She told me nothing! Nothing! My mother's left me stumbling alone through life—
Thomas	You're not alone!
Daniel	Oh, yes. Forgive me! I have an uncle who forgets to meet me at the station, then taunts me with the details of my dead mother's life!
Thomas	You've better friends than that. You've me. And Martha.
Daniel	Then you must tell me what I want to know. How many brothers did my mother have? How did they die?
	Thomas shakes his head warningly at Martha. Again she checks that no one is listening before putting her head close to Daniel's.
Thomas	*[Tensely]* This is a sad long tale I cannot bear to hear again. I'll get about my work.

● ●

SCENE 6

Thomas goes off as Martha and Daniel sit down.

Martha	This house was such a happy place – till Liliana's father fell from his horse and died. We shared two years of tears, then Liliana's mother fell in love with yet another kindly man and married him. He was a widower too, and he came to this house along with his own son, Jack Severn.
Daniel	My uncle? Then the Captain is not my real family?

Martha	Not by blood, no – *[Bitterly]* though he is steeped in it.
Daniel	In blood?
Martha	So I believe. Oh, he can charm the ducks off water when he wants. But we have known your uncle since he was a child. Always he lived on a see-saw. Cheery and open one moment, then in an instant full of spite. Indeed, I recall one of the stable lads saying once, 'Give Jack a stick, and it's the toss of a coin whether he'll use it to beat down weeds or kill his own best friend.' It was as if the devil and an angel wrestled continually for his soul.
Daniel	You think the devil won?
Martha	*[Cautiously peering round again]* I *know* the devil won. First Jolyon died. A happy, chubby fellow. The last child in the world you'd think to come across in his small cot, blue in the face. Then Samuel. We heard the shot in the woods. An accident, they said. But we knew who was in the house and who was not. Then Liliana's mother died, of pains so bad the doctor sent some bumbling arm of the law to peer in the cooking pots.
Daniel	In search of poison?
Martha	Nothing was found. Her kindly husband died of grief. By then, of course, the word was flying round: 'The devil walks up at High Gates'.
Daniel	So many deaths! Did nobody suspect young Jack?
Martha	Oh, yes. But in our fog of grief, the house became a tangle of love and loyalties. I begged my precious Liliana to leave, but she insisted she must stay to watch over her last brother, Edmund. And I believe that Edmund only agreed to go to sea with Jack so he could lure the fiend away from Liliana. And though no one saw what happened one sad night on deck on that short voyage, that was the end of him.
Daniel	All of her brothers dead! And one by one. But surely, once my mother heard the news of Edmund's death—?

ACT 2 SCENE 6

49

Martha	Oh, yes. She fled. That very night, before the fiend came home. Thomas and I crammed everything that Liliana ever cared about onto a cart and sent it off with her, so that, when Jack came home, we could persuade him she'd not fled from him, simply run off to get wed.
Daniel	Why would you tell Jack that?
Martha	We hoped he would not guess that she suspected him. We thought she would be safer. In any case, a letter came a few months later, saying that she had made a truth of our great lie, and wed a gentle husband. And after that, one other letter came, to tell us she had been widowed but she had one comfort in her life. She had a precious son.
Daniel	Me.
Martha	You.
Daniel	You never tried to follow her?
Martha	She never dared to tell us where she was. I think she feared the Captain would prise the information out of us and then find her – and you.
Daniel	*[Puzzled]* But all the time you knew him for a *murderer*.
Martha	Hush! Hush!
Daniel	*[Lowering his voice]* A murderer. But you and Thomas stayed.
Martha	Of course we stayed! Who else would be here, ready to watch over Liliana, should she come back again?
Daniel	But when you learned about my mother's death?
Martha	Why then we knew for *certain* we had to stay – because we knew you would be coming in her place.
Daniel	But Martha, that means I'm next in his sights! He'll want to kill me too. Why, only yesterday he told me he couldn't wait to see me in the Devil Walks! And I have seen that sad, sad line of tombstones. I know what he must mean!
Martha	No, no. He has a reason not to harm you.

Daniel	And what is that?
Martha	You hold the key to finding something that the Captain wants. Something he thinks your mother took away with her. Till he finds that, you're safe. Quite safe!
Captain Severn	*[Off]* Martha! Martha! I need you now!

Martha hurries away.

Daniel	*[To self]* Oh, then, I know the Captain's secret! For all through supper he was pressing me about my mother – and one other thing alone! I could go up into my attic room and write to Dr Marlow – ask for the doll's house to be sent at once – say that I miss it sorely. Then, as the cart carries it up to High Gates, I could make my escape. The Captain would have no reason then to follow me – or wish me further ill.

Daniel turns decidedly towards the house, then hesitates.

But wait! Didn't he do away with baby Jolyon? And Samuel? Edmund. My grandmother, too! So many lives! And even though I didn't know he walked the earth, still, both my mother's life and mine have been thrown from their natural paths by this vile murdering monster. I'll not run back to the Marlows like a frightened child. He'd simply follow me! In any case, how can I leave the mystery like this? Do I not owe it to my mother to find out where the secret lies – and, if I can, avenge her short, unhappy life and her untimely death? Martha assures me I am safe for now. I will believe her! I will find out more!

• •

SCENE 7

In the clearing of the Devil Walks. **Thomas** *is tending the tombstones.* **Daniel** *comes in carrying a note.*

Thomas	What brings you to this gloomy place?
Daniel	While she was shopping, Martha met the carrier. He had this note for you.

| Thomas | *[Unfolding it]* A big delivery expected off the next train. He'll bring it up directly. And I'm to know that he's been told he'll need help to unload it. |
| Daniel | I can be there as well. I'm strong enough. |

Daniel *starts drifting round the stones.*

So now I know these graves. Jolyon, Samuel, my grandmother and her two husbands. And this memorial to Edmund, lost at sea.

Thomas	I see you've tired of all your *cheerful* amusements.
Daniel	No, no. I had a question about another plaything.
Thomas	And what was that?
Daniel	The doll's house. The one my uncle claims went missing when my mother left.
Thomas	*[Sourly]* As well it might, since it was mine to give and hers to take.
Daniel	*[Surprised]* How was it yours to give?
Thomas	Why, boy, I made it! Lord knows, I had enough work of my own. But Liliana begged me over and over until I weakened. It took me four long years, for it was done exactly to please her. 'It must be a perfect model of High Gates itself – down to the last sliding panel and strong coil of ivy.'
Daniel	Why would she care so much?

Thomas	Your mother was a strange soul. Everyone asked her why she had set her favourite gardener a task as long and hard as any in a fairy tale, and she would only say that one day we would understand, because the doll's house, made just so, would save a precious life.
Daniel	How could she know that? Nobody can foretell the future.
Thomas	Your mother had a way of sensing trouble even before it came. She told me once, 'Thomas, I know I shall be loved. But I shall not be happy. And misery and worry will follow me for my whole life.'
Daniel	But she was happy here.
Thomas	Until that black-haired devil came.
Daniel	*Black*-haired? My step-uncle?
Thomas	Jet black. Oh, yes. Look at him now and you'd not recognize him as the same Jack Severn who prowled around this house so restlessly, counting the days till he was old enough to go to sea.
Daniel	He cannot be so old now.
Thomas	No. Some say his hair was bleached by tropic sun. And others whisper that he had a fright so horrid that it turned white overnight.
Daniel	What does *he* say?
Thomas	*[Sourly]* You'll find what the Captain says does not always settle the question. Now off you go. Back to your games and amusements. This is no place for the living.
Daniel	*[To self]* Back to my games? If I were here to pass my days in pleasure and amusement, I'd send for Sophie! No. I stay for one purpose only, and that's to find out how my mother's family were so accursed. Thomas and Martha accuse my step-uncle. And certainly, the man is gruff. But these are manners anyone could learn at sea. And he's been generous, too. Perhaps what the Captain says is right, and Martha and Thomas's wits are as twisted as their spines. For accidents do happen, and grief will always look for somebody to blame. Perhaps in their love for their old family, they wrong the Captain in their bitter accusations.

We hear a distant call.

Thomas	That's Martha, calling. It's the day your uncle settles his accounts. He won't be in the best of tempers. You would be wise not to be late at table!

Daniel runs off.

SCENE 8

*The dining room. Supper is laid. An elated **Captain Severn** is reeling round the table with gleaming eyes and a fiendish grin, as if in some hellish dance. **Daniel** peers round the door.*

Daniel	*[Concerned]* Sir, are you *stung*?
Captain Severn	*[Spinning to a halt]* Stung? No, boy!
Daniel	I saw you dance about. I thought—
Captain Severn	Oh, I will dance! And as for being stung, why you yourself had best take care. More than one thing can sting under this roof.

Captain Severn laughs violently.

Daniel	*[Nervously]* Sir?
Captain Severn	Come in, come in, boy! Oh what a night is this! And what a supper this will be. I'm starved as a bear in spring!

*Captain Severn falls wolfishly on his food. **Daniel** creeps to the table, and keeps his eyes on his plate. **Captain Severn** suddenly stops chewing and eyes **Daniel** coldly.*

So now we play the frightened rabbit, do we?

Daniel	Sir?
Captain Severn	Staring down at your plate like some waif in a poorhouse. *[Banging the table with his fist]* Come, you're a guest under this roof! So sing! Sing for your supper!
Daniel	*[Terrified]* T-t-today— T-today—
Captain Severn	*[Roars]* Yes, sir! Give over stuttering and tell your story *today*!

Daniel	*[Making a massive effort]* Today, I played the bagatelle. Those silver balls are hard to tame. But yet my score was higher than yesterday.
	Captain Severn is staring at him with black hostility.
	[Still terrified] And after that I read a book.
Captain Severn	*[Grimly]* A book. Ha!
Daniel	*[Bravely persisting]* And then I tried again with the big archery bow. My arrows went astray. But by the end of the morning, I'd made a valiant stab at hitting the oak tree.
	Captain Severn's mood switches totally. Now he is grinning madly at Daniel.
Captain Severn	Archery, eh? Then you must let me show you a few tricks!
	Captain Severn sits back, still grinning.
Daniel	*[Still baffled and nervous]* And your own day, sir. Did it go well?
Captain Severn	Go well? *[Again he bangs the table with his fist]* Why, it could not have gone better if I had found a pot of gold at one end of the rainbow!
Daniel	How so?
Captain Severn	*[Dangerously]* Because, sir, I have spied out a *secret*.
Daniel	*[Terrified]* A secret?
Captain Severn	Oh, yes!
	Captain Severn leans threateningly across the table, pointing his knife at Daniel.
	A secret that someone else would no doubt have preferred to keep . . . And why, I ask myself, would anyone try to keep a secret if he did not hope to cheat another?
Daniel	I'm sure I don't know.
Captain Severn	Oh, but I'm sure you *do*.
	There is a long, threatening silence before Captain Severn throws down his napkin.

This meal is *done*. I am away to finish my accounts.

Captain Severn rises. Martha hurries in to clear the plates.

Martha, bring coffee to the study. Something must see me through the next few hours and I assure you that it won't be patience!

Captain Severn stalks out. As Martha piles the plates on her tray, Daniel catches her sleeve.

Daniel	*[Panicking]* Martha, the Captain's seen or heard something to change things. I am sure of it. And I'm not safe to stay. I am away this night! But you must promise you'll come after me. The Marlows are the kindest people. I know that they won't rest till they've found you and Thomas work and shelter.
Martha	No point in running, Daniel.
Daniel	You should have seen his face at supper! I'll be safer gone.
Martha	And just how safe is that? Your mother was pursued into the *grave*. This is no petty wickedness you can escape by running off. This is some deep, deep evil we are dealing with. An evil that has done for one fine boy after another. And for the sweetest lady who ever lived, and her one gentle daughter. Surely you understand that if you are to live the rest of your life in any sort of peace or safety, you must be rid of what hangs over you.
Daniel	You've done your best for me, I know. And I am grateful. But the man is in some strange and twisted frenzy. I would be safer gone this very night. Here, I am like a rabbit in a cage!
Martha	We have had those before, and set them free. Now calm yourself. The Captain has been penned in his study settling his accounts all day, and will be there for hours yet. His temper is uncertain. I'll make his coffee. And you must pay his mood no mind. It's my belief he frightens you tonight only for his amusement.

Martha hurries off.

Daniel	For his amusement! Why then the man's a very fiend! I'm glad he's penned up safely with his accounts! *[Pause]* Penned up? *[Daniel points to the side]* There, in his study. *[He points upwards]* And there, above me, is the room where the Captain

sleeps. The only room I haven't seen. Martha says I'll not live in peace and safety until I find the evil that hangs over me and root it out. Suppose the secret's there?

Daniel *creeps to the study door and listens.*

I hear his angry mutterings. So if I plan to leave tonight, here is a chance I cannot miss. *[Pointing]* I must go up there. And I must do it now.

• •

SCENE 9

The Captain's private room. It's cluttered with worn furniture, an untidy desk, a globe, binoculars, piles of maps and papers, a stuffed parrot, a witch doctor's mask, a handful of souvenir arrows in a jar, a cutlass, a ship in a bottle, etc. On the wall hangs an impressive portrait of a man in his twenties wearing naval dress uniform. It can barely be seen because the floor to ceiling drapes are drawn across, leaving it in shadow.

Daniel

[Entering] So here's his room. A window on his life. Are these the treasures he brought home with him? What's in this jar? Are these the very poison darts that flew at him? And did he dare to snatch them up as he ran? *[**Daniel** runs his fingers over a dart, then freezes, realizing there might still be poison on its tip]* I look at these marvels and think perhaps I wrong him in believing Martha's grim tales. Here is a man who led a life of great alarms and fine adventures. Who would expect him to be soft as butter, or full of patience with a young nephew he thinks still wet behind the ears?

Daniel draws back the drapes.

And he has told me such fine tales on our long walks together. See? There's the parrot who learned to imitate his voice so well, and took to ordering the sailors up and down the ropes till they were dizzy. *[Wistfully]* If I could trust him, why, I might even copy him and go to sea myself! After so thin a life as mine, I'd cherish the chance to see such wonders.

Daniel turns round and sees the portrait.

I'd look like that! Full fledged in uniform, looking so strong and brave. Is that the Captain when he was just young Jack? Oh, Thomas was right to call his hair jet black. He was a handsome man when he was young. *[Suddenly puzzled]* And yet . . . And yet . . . There is a look about him that I recognize. And not just the same face aged, with snow-white hair. I've seen this very likeness before . . .

*Stepping closer, **Daniel** accidentally knocks two loose pages off the desk onto the floor and hastily picks them up.*

Strange! Here is a letter in dear Sophie's handwriting. *[Turns one page over]* And it's to me. But it's been opened and read. Why should my step-uncle not have given it me directly? *[Reading aloud]* 'And so, dear Daniel, I cannot bear to have that horrid two-headed doll under our roof a moment longer. I swear he stares at me. Sometimes he smirks. And always he poisons all my games. I lock him in the box, and in an instant Mama has found some reason to send me to my room. It is as if that fiendish little sprite has powers to punish me with some small shade of what is done to him. So I have begged and begged. And Father has at last sent for the carrier, who will take the doll's house to the train, and on to High Gates. It will be with you directly.'

Daniel *lets the letter drop. Slowly, he turns to stare at the portrait again.*

Of course! The double-headed doll! So Thomas did not only make the doll's house. He whittled the dolls as well! Wasn't my mother's family likeness quite plain to Sophie when she called Mrs Golightly Mrs Cunningham? And Thomas must have carved Jack as a boy and a man. That is the doll the Captain seeks. That is his heart's desire! The evil and enchanted mirror image he hopes will make his future. What did he tell me? Some horrid witch doctor will give it secret powers and after that you're intertwined till death. Torment the doll and you will writhe in misery. Shower favours on it and you'll thrive. This is what he has waited for so long. And now he knows that it is on its way.

Daniel *turns to the window. He points.*

And, see! Those tiny puffs of smoke between the downs. The train is on its way with its delivery. My secret's out! I am a dead boy now!

The door flies open. **Captain Severn** *stands in the doorway with an evil grin.*

Captain Severn   [*Sarcastically*] Smart boy! Smart boy! I do believe that, like your mother, you can predict your future.

Darkness

ACT 3

SCENE 1

*An attic room. We hear the thumping and kicking as **Captain Severn** drags **Daniel** up the last of the stairs.*

Daniel	*[Off]* Stop, stop! Let go of me! I will not do it! I will not write a letter.

Captain Severn pushes Daniel roughly into the room and hurls a few sheets of paper and a pen in after him.

Captain Severn *[Teasing]* Come, come! The easiest of tasks! A farewell note to me, blessing your dear, dear uncle for his great kindness and telling me that, fired by my own fine example, you're off to sea. Oh, yes. I think the Marlows will be pleased to read it when I visit them. It will console them – after you're never seen again!

Daniel hurls himself towards the door.

Daniel I'll never do it. Never!

Captain Severn pushes him back.

Captain Severn *[Venomously]* Then you must stay here till you starve or rot. But be assured that, one way or another, I'll tip your bones into the Devil Walks.

Daniel You will be found out! Martha and Thomas will search for me!

Captain Severn Martha and Thomas? Why, now my precious doll is on its way, I have no further need of those two fools. I am away right now to send them packing and to dig your grave. So write your letter, boy, before I hurry back and *make* you!

Captain Severn slams the door. We hear a bolt drawn across.

Daniel My God! I am in trouble! A rat in a trap!

Daniel rattles the door. He rushes to the window and peers down.

Mercy! The drop! And not a handhold in sight. *[Peering to both sides]* Wait! There, at the corner of the house, the ivy coils up to the roof! But it's too far away for me to reach. No. Hopeless! Hopeless! *[Sitting on the edge of the bed]* So must I end my life as it began, on a bed in a tiny room? Small wonder that my mother hid me away so well! Oh, now I know how evil that man is, I can forgive her. I can forgive her *everything*. A wretched choice! For all those years she must have hated seeing me lying a-bed like that. She was not cruel. No, she was not unkind. She loved me utterly. And all she wanted was to save my precious life!

Daniel drops his head in his hands. There is a moment of silence. Then he raises it again.

'A precious life' . . .? I hear it like an echo. Why is that? *[He stands]* Of course! It is what Thomas said. That she insisted that the doll's house be a true model 'so one day it would save a precious life'. 'It must be perfect', she told him, 'down to the last sliding panel and coil of ivy'.

Daniel rushes to the wall.

Here is where Sophie found a way to push her pirate doll through, up to the roof and safety. Can it be true? Is there some sliding place? *[He runs his hands over the wall]* Nothing. No, I am lost. But, wait! What's this? A hole as tiny as a woodworm's passage. Is there some cunning spring hidden inside? No way to reach it. Here's my stubby finger, and there's the hole, no bigger than a stitch in lace! *[He frowns]* A stitch in lace!

Daniel digs in his pocket and draws out his mother's lace-making tool case.

My mother sends her blessings from the grave! *[Spilling the tools in his hand]* This one! It could be made for the task! *[He pushes it in place]* A click! I hear a click!

Daniel *slides the panel aside.*

Light! I see light pouring through cracked roof tiles. Now I can reach the roof! Those coils of ivy! They were sturdy enough when Thomas made the doll's house. They will be strong as iron now. I must be brave. If Simple Jack can clamber down a beanstalk in a fairy tale, then so can I to save my life!

Daniel *takes one last look around the room, takes a deep breath and plunges through the hole in the wall.*

• •

SCENE 2

A courtyard. ***Daniel*** *is clinging to the ivy that climbs up the side of the house. Dropping to the ground, he flattens his back against the wall as he peers cautiously around. Far in the distance we hear the whistle of a train and the sound of a cart in the distance.*

Daniel   I hear the pony cart. It's getting closer. Now is my chance to run.

Captain Severn *steps out of his side of the house. The two cannot see one another.* ***Captain Severn*** *is alternately shading his eyes to see into the distance and pacing impatiently.*

Captain Severn   I hear the carrier's cart. My heart's desire! On its way back to me at last. Oh, hurry! Hurry!

Daniel   *[Peering around the corner of the house]* My step-uncle! He cannot wait to get that evil little manikin back in his life. Well, let him! Let him!

Daniel *starts to run the other way, then stops.*

How can I go? How can I leave like this? For even locked away this hateful sprite had the worst powers. Pinned down inside its tiny coffin space inside the doll's house, its poisonous spirit still managed to seep into our lives. It turned my mother's mind, and made her change from the warm, open Liliana everybody knew into some stiff, pale mockery of her real self. And she had fought with all her strength against my uncle's bad intent.

The cart is getting closer.

Captain Severn	*[In rapture]* Oh, hurry! Hurry! Come back to me!
Daniel	The danger! Why, even gentle Sophie could be changed by this vile doll – turning into a vengeful monster in our games – spitting out horrid voices.
Captain Severn	How many years have we been forced to wait! What plans I've hatched! At last our moment comes!

In a frenzy **Captain Severn** *pushes back his hair to reveal a scar.*

Daniel	Is that a *scar* under his hair? Were he and the doll made *twins* in *evil*, linked for life, that Sophie's carelessness to one could scar the other in the selfsame place?

Captain Severn *throws himself on his knees and clasps his hands.*

Captain Severn	Come back to me! Come back!
Daniel	What did the vicar say? 'The devil walks. But he can make no headway till we invite him in.' And now the Captain *begs* the doll to come.
Captain Severn	We have been parted all too long! Oh, hurry back!
Daniel	He is in rapture! Oh, now I fear it's true. Once in my uncle's hands – once evil has joined hands with evil – what might not happen? No! I must get to the cart before it reaches him.

Daniel *runs off. We hear the frantic neighing of a horse.*

• •

SCENE 3

A corner of the courtyard. **Thomas** *and* **Martha** *are shuffling across, each carrying a carpet bag and a few sad possessions, two rusty saucepans, a kettle,* **Thomas**'s *rake and spade.* **Daniel** *hurries in with the box of dolls and dumps it on the ground.*

Martha	That box! I recognize that box.
Carrier	*[Following **Daniel** in]* Hey, boy! Don't rush away with one small part of the load. I need some help to get this bulky doll's house off the cart.
Martha	*[Clutching her heart]* The doll's house? Liliana's doll's house? It's back again?
Thomas	It's of no consequence to us. Not any more. *[Sourly, to the **Carrier**]* Go ask the Captain. He'll find he cannot order a workman off his land and then expect his help.
	*The **Carrier** goes off. **Martha** and **Thomas** watch as **Daniel** wrenches up the box lid. He spills the contents on the ground, and pounces on the two-headed doll.*
Daniel	*[Holding it up]* So there you are, you evil little creature! On which dark voyage did my uncle carry you ashore and barter with the witch doctor to cast a spell? How much blood was there spilled? How much gold paid? Small wonder you're so precious to the Captain! That's why he hid you so well when he went off to murder Edmund. And why he was so wild with rage to find you gone when he came home.

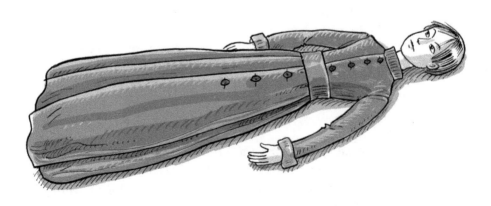

Thomas	Daniel, you lose your wits. A doll is just a doll. It has no strength of purpose.
Daniel	You're wrong. This little manikin can make things happen. And once it's in my uncle's grasp, the evil will swing round to face its own true north. It's home to work its master's will and wreak his horrid vengeance on the world. He'll harness all its force and scatter devilry into a far, far grander orbit than this sad house.

Daniel shakes the doll in the air.

All of this trouble! All of this pain and misery! These ruined lives! All of it springs from you!

The doll jerks itself out of Daniel's grasp. As Thomas and Martha stare in horror, it slides across the floor.

Martha	Oh, mercy! The thing lives!
Thomas	It moves. The boy is right. It is bewitched! Oh, horror!
Captain Severn	*[Roaring, off]* Where is my doll? Where is my doll? Someone has stolen it from its hiding place! Carrier! Have you been thieving?
Carrier	*[Backing on to the stage away from Captain Severn]* Not I, sir! No! I have not touched your load!

The doll jerks itself towards Captain Severn's voice.

Daniel	No, no! You will not reach him! You will not!

Daniel pulls out his mother's lace-making tools. He approaches the doll with one in his hand.

Captain Severn	*[Enters, roaring with rage]* Where is my doll? Where is my doll? *[Seeing Daniel]* What? Has the boy become a *rat*, to slip away through walls? Where is my doll?

The doll jerks closer to Captain Severn.

Captain Severn	*[Triumphantly]* Aha!
Daniel	*[To the doll]* No! You'll not go to him!

*Daniel stabs the doll through the heart then hurls it to the side of the house as **Captain Severn** clutches his own heart and staggers.*

Captain Severn   No, no! Not me! Not me! This is not how we are supposed to be entwined! Oh, God! My heart! Not me! Not me!

*Captain Severn staggers more, then drops. **Thomas**, **Martha**, **Daniel** and the **Carrier** nervously draw closer.*

Thomas   What, is he dead?

Carrier   *[Feeling for a heartbeat]* Stone dead. Felled by his own black wrath.

Daniel   More by his own black venom! Their souls were twinned right to the very last. He's shared the foul doll's fate.

Carrier   His eyes stare out as if he saw into the very pit of hell.

Daniel   And there he'll burn.

*They stand around the **Captain**'s body. Nobody notices that a little spiral of smoke has begun to rise above the doll lying against the wall.*

Thomas   *[To the **Carrier**]* You'll take his body to the town for us?

Carrier   I will. Come, boy, and help me get the doll's house off the cart to make a space.

*Smoke begins to rise more thickly from the doll as, one by one, they trudge offstage, leaving the body of **Captain Severn**. There is a tiny burst of flame.*

• •

SCENE 4

*In the grounds of High Gates. We see the reflected red and orange flickering of a great fire. **Martha** is sitting on an upturned wheelbarrow or half barrel. **Thomas** and **Daniel** stand beside her, in front of a group of **Villagers**, who are all pointing and whispering excitedly as they watch the house burn. We hear the crackle of fire and sharp explosive sounds like cap shots firing.*

Villager 1   See how the fire rises! Such a sight!

Villager 2	The chandelier. Hear how each crystal drop explodes like gunfire!
Villager 3	Stand clear! There goes another beam!
	The Villagers shuffle back.
Villager 1	Who would have thought live ivy could burn so fast?
Villager 3	That house won't last another hour.
	4th Villager comes in shaking his head sadly. He whispers something to the villagers behind Daniel.
Daniel	*[Overhearing]* What? Is the doll's house burned to ashes too? *[Daniel turns to Thomas]* Oh, Thomas!
Thomas	It's for the best. I sometimes think that it is only fire that knows how to take leave of the past, and face the future cleanly. *[Waving a hand towards the fire]* Will you rebuild?
Daniel	*[Confused]* Rebuild?
Thomas	High Gates is yours now – what is left of it.
Daniel	Mine?
Thomas	Whose else?
	Thomas turns to talk to the villagers. Daniel wanders aside.
Daniel	*[To self]* Will I stay? No. I'll go home! *[Pause]* Did I say 'home'? How much has wheeled about in these last months! The word no longer conjures up a picture of my mother sitting by my bed in that small room. No. Now I see an airy house cluttered with bonnets and ribbons, bursting with merriment and laughter.
	Daniel hurries to Thomas and tugs at his sleeve.
	No, I'll not stay here. I'll go back. Back to the Marlows. And you and Martha must come with me, for a better life.
Thomas	No, no. You can't uproot old stock. Martha and I are far too old to start our lives again. *[Thinking]* But she and I could make a living on this land.

Daniel	I'm pleased to hear it. Do as you both think fit. Treat the place as your own.
Thomas	And maybe you'll come back one day?
Daniel	*[Dubiously]* Perhaps. *[He gathers confidence]* Perhaps, yes. And I'll build a fine new house fit for the wife I hope to find, and all the children we'll have. Children who'll tumble round these gardens as happily as Liliana and her brothers did before Jack Severn came.
Thomas	*[Smiling]* A fine and happy future.
Martha	Yes. A fine and happy future. One that would give your mother joy to see.
Daniel	Yes, one that will give her joy to see. And I can think of her with love again. And she can rest in peace.

Thomas puts one arm round Martha as she blots her tears. He slides the other round Daniel's shoulders as the three of them turn back in silence to watch the fire.

There is a prolonged sound of cracking timbers and a shower of sparks.

Blackout

ACTIVITIES

1 A GOTHIC TALE

Anne Fine, the author of *The Devil Walks*, describes the story as 'a gothic tale . . . a brooding and malevolent chiller thriller'.

In pairs, talk about what you understand about the terms 'gothic' and 'malevolent' (use the clues and a dictionary if necessary), then share your ideas with the class.

> The word 'malevolent' comes from two Latin words:
> *mal* = bad or harm
> *volens* = wishing

> The stories of *Frankenstein* and *Dracula* are typical gothic tales. They were both written in the 19th century, when gothic novels were extremely popular.

Below are some key features often found in gothic tales:

graves
dark, mysterious buildings
secrets
fear
madness
grief
danger
coffins
ghosts
isolated, overgrown or neglected places
evil
blood
death
a malevolent character
an object with strange power or influence
a battle between good and evil
savage animals
a hero or heroine

1. In small groups, decide which of the features opposite are included in *The Devil Walks* and list them.

2. Divide up the listed features among the people in your group. Each person should consider how their features are used in the playscript. For example:
   - when and where it appears in the play
   - what effect it has on the plot or characters
   - what effect it creates for the reader (e.g. it makes them feel curious, puzzled, excited, suspicious, tense, sympathy, etc.).

3. In your group, take turns to explain a feature, until all the features have been covered.

4. Imagine your group has been asked to design a poster to advertise the play. Sketch out some possible designs, including gothic images. Think carefully about:
   - colours
   - mood
   - lettering style
   - how to catch people's attention and make them want to see the play!

Assessment

- **Self-assessment.** Think carefully about how well you worked with your group. Give yourself a thumbs up 👍 or thumbs down 👎 as to whether you did the following:
  - listened carefully to what other people said
  - gave good reasons if you disagreed with something
  - gave your own ideas clearly and in detail.

- **Peer assessment.** Ask the rest of the class to comment on your poster ideas. Ask them to comment on two things they like about it and one thing they think could be improved.

2 BREAKING NEWS

The 'whisperings of all the ladies in the town' result in Doctor Marlow visiting Hawthorn Cottage. This leads to the discovery of Daniel and the taking away of his mother.

In small groups, imagine you are part of a local TV news group. You have been asked to report on the events in the village.

1. Choose one person to be the main reporter and others to be witnesses who give brief interviews (e.g. Dr Marlow, Daniel, some of the Gossips, Mrs Cunningham).

2. Plan how you will introduce the story. Think about:
    ● when
    ● where
    ● how
    ● why
    ● who.

3. Draw up questions to ask the people you want to interview. Try to make them open-ended questions, so the person does not just answer 'Yes' or 'No'.

4. Think carefully about how you will role-play the characters. How might they speak? What might they be feeling? Would they give interviews reluctantly or enthusiastically? Try to convey the characters and their emotions through what they say, their expressions, gestures and body language.

5. Conduct your interviews. If possible, record it so you can play it back afterwards. Some sentence starters that your interviewees might use are given on the opposite page.

6. In pairs, write a news article for the local newspaper. You can re-use information from your TV report and interviews. Remember to include:

- a headline
- a summary of events
- quotations from people involved
- speculation as to what might happen next
- a photo (a rough sketch will do) and a caption.

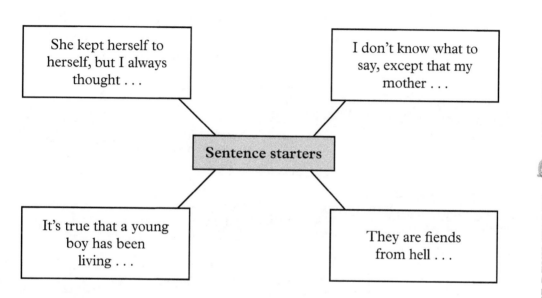

ASSESSMENT

- **Self-assessment.** Consider how well you performed in the role play. Rate yourself on a scale of 1 to 3, with 3 being the highest. How well did you:
  - stay in character throughout the interview?
  - show what your character was like through your voice, gestures and expressions?
  - answer the questions fully and in detail?

- **Teacher assessment.** Invite your teacher to comment on which group produced the most effective interview and the best news article, and to explain why.

3 SECLUDED OR ENTOMBED?

Anne Fine keeps the reader in suspense about her characters. Like Daniel, we are puzzled by his mother's behaviour. Our ideas about her change as the plot develops.

1. Below are some quotations from characters about Liliana Cunningham. With a partner, work out who said what, and when. If necessary, look back through the playscript.

'I think my mother is a quiet woman.'

'the rest of the town says your mother is insane.'

'Her mind is hectic . . . it hovers on a knife edge'

'I cannot help but feel she did me terrible wrong to keep me locked away.'

'Liliana was a lively child . . . Talkative. Merry.'

'my poor dear sister and her pitiful life'

'I can think of her with love again. And she can rest in peace.'

2. When Daniel learns about his mother's happy, active childhood, he is puzzled and upset. In Act 2, Scene 5, he says:

'Here's a mystery. Can one person truly be two? ... How can I love her memory the way I would, when everywhere I look shows me she knew what childhood happiness should be? And yet, to me, she offered only a small back room and one long lie. And that was cruel.'

Imagine that Liliana knew Daniel might question her behaviour one day, so she wrote a letter or left a recording for her son, explaining why she acted as she did.

Either write that letter, or make a recording. Remember:
- You are speaking/writing as Liliana, so use the first person ('I' or 'we').
- Start and finish your work in an appropriate way.
- Give some facts but also explain your feelings.
- Try to give Daniel some reassurance and advice for his future.

Share your letter or recording with the rest of the class.

3. In pairs, discuss whether Liliana was right to try and keep Daniel away from the world. Was he 'entombed' or just 'secluded'? Talk about what might have happened to Daniel if he hadn't been spotted in the garden by the Gossips. As a pair, decide whether you think, on balance, Liliana did the right thing. Share your ideas with the rest of the class and take a vote on whether Daniel was 'secluded' or 'entombed'.

ASSESSMENT

- **Self-assessment.** Assess how well you completed the writing task using traffic-light marking, i.e. green for 'very well', amber for 'quite well' and red for 'not well at all'.

- **Peer assessment.** Feedback on a partner's letter or recording. Comment on how well they:
    - kept using the first person
    - explained why they acted as they did
    - sounded convincing and full of care for Daniel.

4 THE DOLL'S HOUSE

In a review of the novel (on which this playscript is based), another author, Mal Peet, talks about the role of the doll's house in the story. He explains:

> 'There is little for Daniel to inherit, other than a very large, exquisitely made doll's house – a fastidious* scale model of the great house in which Liliana grew up. This doll's house is **the engine of the story.** It is also **its driving metaphor,** for this plaything has a hidden and evil inhabitant.'

* very careful about small details

1. What do you think Mal Peet means by the two phrases in bold? With a partner, look at the opinions below and decide whether you agree or disagree with them. Share your choices with another pair and explain your reasons.

I think Mal Peet thinks of the house as a sort of vehicle, which moves and takes the plot in a new direction.

I think Mal Peet believes there is an old-fashioned engine hidden in the house somewhere.

I think Mal Peet thinks that the doll's house is a metaphor because it represents something much greater and bigger than itself.

I think Mal Peet uses the word 'driving' to emphasize how powerful and controlling the doll's house and its 'inhabitants' are.

2. You could say that the role of the doll's house in *The Devil Walks* is just as important as any of the characters. In pairs or small groups, list the ways that the doll's house is important to the story and moves it along. Here are some ideas to get you started:

> It is Daniel's only toy at Hawthorn Cottage.

> It is the only link Daniel has with his mother's past.

> It is the focus of games Daniel shares with Sophie.

3. Liliana told Daniel that one day the doll's house would 'save a precious life'. In pairs draw a sketch or perform a scene to show how the doll's house saved Daniel's life. (Think about what Sophie discovered when she was playing with the doll's house, and how Daniel used that knowledge later.)

ASSESSMENT

- **Self-assessment.** Rate yourself from 1 to 3 (with 3 being the highest) on how well you did in the following tasks:
  - explained what you thought Mal Peet meant by his references to the doll's house in his review
  - contributed to the list of ways the doll's house is important in the play
  - illustrated how the doll's house 'saved a precious life'.

- **Peer assessment.** Ask your partner how well you:
  - listened to his or her ideas
  - explained your own ideas
  - worked together on the sketch or performance.

5 FREEZE FRAMES

In small groups, present three freeze frames to the rest of the class. Ask your classmates to try to guess which moments in the play are being shown.

To prepare for this activity:

Choose three moments in the play to present.

Decide who will play which character in the frame. (Note that you cannot use any props in your freeze frame.)

Arrange the characters as if they have been frozen in the middle of a performance. (Think about how they might stand, sit or lie, their expressions, their gestures, eye contact with each other, whether they are speaking, etc.)

Each character must consider carefully what they would be thinking and feeling. (They may be questioned.)

Present your freeze frames, allowing enough time for a member of the audience to tap one character on the shoulder to hear their thoughts and feelings.

Ask the class to guess the moment in the play, name the characters taking part and describe what is being shown.

Assessment

- **Self-assessment.** Think about how you worked in the group. Give yourself a mark from 1 to 3 (3 being the highest) for:
    - how well you contributed to the group's choices
    - how well you listened to others' ideas
    - how well you held your role in the freeze frame.

- **Peer assessment.** Ask the class for feedback on your freeze frames. Invite them to comment on what you did well. Then ask for suggestions as to how you could improve your frames. Encourage other students to swap roles to see how their suggestions might work.

6 IMPROVISE A SCENE

In Act 2, Scene 9, Daniel goes into his uncle's room, which he describes as a 'window on his life'. What he sees impresses him and he briefly wonders if he has misjudged his uncle.

Imagine what might have happened if Daniel hadn't found Sophie's letter. If Captain Severn had just found Daniel full of admiration for his past adventures, would he still have tried to kill him? Or might he have tried to make Daniel his ally in his future plans?

In small groups of three or four, improvise an alternative scene.

You might want to use some of the following ideas to prepare for your new scene:

If Daniel asked his uncle to tell him about the things in the room, how might the captain react? Would he be flattered? Nostalgic? Boastful?

What effect might these tales have on Daniel?

How might the captain turn Daniel against Martha, Thomas, the Marlows and his mother?

Who else might enter the scene?

Would the captain still try to kill Daniel?

Might Daniel be tempted by the power of voodoo?

What might the captain do or say to make Daniel change his mind again?

In your groups, talk about some different ideas and work towards a general agreement about how to play the scene. Then perform the scene in front of the class. After discussion, you may wish to amend the scene and then write it down as a script.

ASSESSMENT

- **Self-assessment.** Give yourself a thumbs up 👍 or a thumbs down 👎 for how well you did in the following aspects of the task:
  - suggesting ideas to the rest of the group
  - listening carefully to other people's ideas
  - responding to the other actors in the scene
  - playing the role of your chosen character.

- **Peer assessment.** Invite feedback from the rest of the class on your improvisation. Ask them to comment on four things that worked well and two things that could be improved upon.

7 PORTRAITS IN WORDS

In the novel, the portrait of his uncle makes a strong impression on Daniel. When he pulls back the curtains the sunlight falls on the painting.

> 'There the captain stood in full dress uniform, the Severin doll, with that familiar face smirking contemptuously [. . .] How well I knew that haughty, taunting and malevolent smile that had tormented me so often over my supper.'
> (page 232)

Imagine Daniel did build a new house on the land at High Gates, and rescued some old portraits from the fire. He may have married one of the Marlow sisters and had his own family. Many years later, you inherit the house and find portraits of all the characters in this story hanging in one of the rooms. Some look newer than others; they have obviously been painted at different times.

1. Choose one portrait to describe. You need to decide:
   - who is in the painting
   - when it was done (so how old the character is and what has happened to them)
   - the style of artwork (e.g. a traditional oil painting, or a modern impression)
   - what sort of frame it is in.

   Think carefully about:
   - your overall impression of the person
   - details of what they are wearing, where they are, how they are posed
   - any background details which might hint at a hobby or interest or work
   - a clear description of their expression and posture, and what these might say about their character.

Remember that you do not know the people in the pictures, but a good artist would be able to convey the character's personality and some of their history through their portrait.

You might find one of these sentence starters helpful:

The young Victorian woman gazing out of the portrait had intelligent, lively eyes, although there was a hint of anxiety . . .

A care-worn, creased, but kindly face was smiling . . .

The gentleman stood formally beside the gate-post . . .

A young mother looked down fondly at the small child clutching her hand . . .

2. When you have finished writing your first draft, give it to a partner and ask them to comment on:
   - who they think it is
   - when the portrait was painted (and what might have happened to them)
   - how well you have conveyed their personality.

3. Using your partner's comments, write a final description of your portrait, proof-reading for any grammar, spelling or punctuation mistakes.

ASSESSMENT

- **Self-assessment.** Assess how well you conveyed your chosen character through your description of their portrait, using traffic-light marking, i.e. green for 'very well', amber for 'quite well' and red for 'not well at all'. Think about the following aspects:
  - the physical detail of their clothing
  - their facial expression and posture
  - how clearly you conveyed a sense of their personality and history.

- **Teacher assessment.** Ask your teacher to choose two or three portrait descriptions to read out to the class and to comment on how well the writer has 'portrayed' their subject.

FURTHER ACTIVITIES

. . . .

1. Write the advertisement that Dr Marlow may have put in the magazine, along with his daughter's painting of the doll's house.

2. Plan a trailer for a film version of *The Devil Walks*. You will need to introduce the story and include some snapshot scenes from the play. Think about how to use music and lighting to convey the mood of a chiller thriller.

3. Write a 'tweet' to summarize the story of *The Devil Walks* (you can use up to 140 characters, including spaces).

4. Write Daniel's diary entry for the night of the fire. Include details of what happened as well as Daniel's thoughts and feelings, and hopes for the future.

5. Find some music or songs that you think might be suitable as part of a soundtrack for a film version of this story. Think about how to convey different feelings for different parts of the story, e.g. tension and suspense, drama, fury, sadness, peace.

6. Make a brief video recording (maybe on a mobile phone) introducing the story to someone who doesn't know it, and explaining what the title, *The Devil Walks*, means.

7. With a partner, write a definition of the term 'voodoo' as you understand it. Then compare it to a dictionary definition.